WISDOMS BY DOROTHY

Dorothy Sweet Calhoun, Author

I HAVE BEEN WRITING FOR TEN YEARS.
WRITING HAS BEEN A GREAT ADVENTURE IN MY
LIFE SINCE RETIREMENT
HAVING SERVED MY SCHOOL DISTRICT AS A
TEACHER AND ASSISTANT PRINCIPAL.

I HAVE WRITTEN AND PUBLISHED THREE CHILDREN'S BOOKS:

Why Dinosaurs Are Extinct

The Princesses of Arvallay: A Multicultural Celebration

Six Bees for Children: A Collection of Educational Wisdoms

RECENT EDUCATION BOOK: **School Behavioral Issues in the USA**

Dorothy

INTRODUCTION / PURPOSE

This book is a collection of "Pearls of Wisdom" gathered over the years from notable persons and leaders such as, workshop facilitators, business persons, public and motivational speakers, friends, and many, many wise Ministers I have met and have known.

Too, there are credited quotes from very famous persons and celebrities that I admire, but have never met.

We are released from any copyright infringement of any persons quoting from any writer's collection of published materials. We have no knowledge of it.

Sometimes, one might need a short, cute, effective way to respond to another individual or group on special occasions. Well, this book would be the answer to meet that need. It can provide just the right touch of humor or wisdom one might need.

Finally, one may use this book of wisdoms for personal enjoyment, for special occasions, for business functions, or as a terrific gift for another.   ENJOY!!

Wisdoms

Life Quotes

"Troubles don't last always, but just long enough for you to learn what you need to learn." Dr. Denny Davis, Pastor, St. John Church Unleashed, Grand Prairie, TX, 7/24/11

"I'm Hyena Happy and Peacock Proud!" Rev. James Davis, St. John Church Unleashed, Grand Prairie, TX, 5/3/14

"What will I do with my OVERTIME?"

"Life doesn't have to make sense to me for life to work and for me to participate in it."

"People who cannot change cannot grow." Rev. James Thomas, Rhema Word Church, Dallas, TX

"I'm just a country boy turned loose in the *city*!" Rev. James Davis, Grand Prairie, TX, 3/11/12

"It's alright to be a copy cat. Just copy the right cat!" Bishop Walter S. Thomas, Louisville, KY, 10/18/11

"When you *don't* do the things you are suppose to do, you will be *forced* to do things you don't want to do," Rev. Terry Anderson, 3/5/14

"Everybody in your camp is not in your corner." Rev. Jeremy Upton, Miami, FL, 7/14/13

"You can't park by your past, move forward!" Dr. Denny Davis, 6/1/14

"We cannot let what surrounds us define us." Dr. Denny Davis, 6/1/14

"It is sad when bad decisions are made in the face of good information."

"I'm precious cargo on the sea of life's journey."

"Where there is no deposit, there will be no withdrawal." Rev. Robert L. White, Grand Prairie, TX

"If your bell isn't ringing, your clap is broken." Dr. E.V. Hill, TBN, 6/5/94

"We must live in the house we build." Dr. Charles Stanley, 1/31/93

"Watch out how you S-T-R-E-T-C-H the truth; it could S-N-A-P back at you!" H. Lesman

"Academic Emphasis = Focuses on content – not football."

"Some people let their *position* mess up their *disposition*." Rev. C.L. Price, 4/25/89

"You must stand for something, or you will stand for anything." Rev. Bradford, Sunset Baptist Church, Grand Prairie, TX, 11/18/90

"What time is it? Don't check your watch, check your life!" Romans 13:11-12, Rev. W.E. McGruder, Progressive Baptist Church, Sherman, Texas, 11/22/92

"Procrastination is a thief of time." Rev. W.E. McGruder, Progressive Baptist Church, Sherman, TX, 11/22/92

"If everything seems to be coming your way, you're probably in the wrong lane." H. Lesman

"When you have accumulated sufficient knowledge to get by, you're too old to remember it!" H. Lesman

"An adult is someone who has stopped growing except in the middle." H. Lesman

"There's nothing more frightening than ignorance in action." Dottie Jones, 7/25/93

"Life is what happens to you when you are making other plans." Betty Talmadge

"You can't be brave if you've only had wonderful things happen to you." Mary Tyler Moore

"It is hard to fight an enemy who has outposts in your head." Sally Kempton

"Good instincts usually tell you what to do long before your head has figured it out." Michael Burke

"The 6 most important words are - I admit I made a mistake; The 5 most important words are - You did a good job; The 4 most important words are – What is your opinion? The 3 most important words are – If you please; The 2 most important words are – Thank you; and the least important word is 'I'." David Weiss

"If you want something said, ask a man; if you want something done, ask a woman." Margaret Thatcher

"Whatever women do they must do twice as well as men to be thought half as good. luckily, this is not difficult." Charlotte Whitton

"If you wait, all that happens is that you get older." Larry McMurtry

"You may be disappointed if you fail, but you are doomed if you don't try." Beverly Sills

"In youth, we learn; in age, we understand." Marie Ebner-Eschenbach

"Forget the Joneses. You can't keep up anyway!!"

"Read carefully anything that requires your signature. Remember, big print giveth and the small print taketh away." H. Brown, Jr.

"Then – if the 'HAVES' HAVE, they should make sure that the 'HAVE NOTS' HAVE." Rev. Robert L. White, 8/25/87

"If you are out of business, take your sign down!" Rev. Robert L. White, 1992

"Spite is never lonely. Envy always tags along." H. Lesman

"You can't have everything! Where would you put it?" H. Lesman

"Everything is 48 and 2 = Means everything is okay." Mr. Charlie Aiken, Zwolle, Louisiana

"Looking through the rock." Mr. John Odom, Odom's
Barbeque/Café, Zwolle, Louisiana

"Hot darn – the – luck!" Jack Sweet, St. John Church, Zwolle,
Louisiana, 1950

**"There are special people who come into our
lives to teach us, support us, encourage us, and
to love us. They leave their imprints on our
hearts and we will never be the same again."**
Lionel Ritchie

**"We are not interested in the possibilities of
defeat."** Queen Elizabeth

**"Opportunities are usually disguised by hard
work, so most people don't recognize them."** Ann
Landers

**"Be the first to climb the highest haystack, jump!
And if you fall, dust yourself off and try again. If
you break your arm, it will heal. Learn how to
prevent such an error, but never stop jumping."**
Dorothy Gregg

"You can't shake hands with a clenched fist."
Indira Gandhi

"Being powerful is like being a lady. If you have to tell people you are, you aren't." Margaret Thatcher

"From birth to age 18, a girl needs good parents. From 18 to 38, she needs good love
From 38 to 55, she needs a good
Personality.
And from 55 on she needs cash!!"
Sophie Tucker

"Treat people as if they were what they ought to be and you help them become what they are capable of becoming." Goethe

"There are only 2 kinds of people who fail: Those who listen to nobody and those who listen to everybody." H. Lesman

"Wine has 9 fights and 7 arguments in it!" Rev. Ollie McDade, Ennis, TX, 1/11/95

"It's hard to be *BIG* when *little* has you!" Bishop T.D. Jakes, 9/22/15

"*Ungrateful*: The bird was freezing. A cow dropped hot manure to thaw it. It thawed and complained. A cat heard him complain and ate the bird.
Lesson: Everyone who drops manure on you is not your enemy; every one is not your friend; keep your mouth shut when you are in manure!" Rev. Daryl Atkinson, St. John Church Unleashed, Grand Prairie, TX, 10/23/11

"A penny for your thoughts: If it does not make 'CENTS,' it does not make 'DOLLARS.'" Dr. Denny Davis, 2/2/14

"When you experience racism, don't let it make you *BITTER*, but let it make you *BETTER*!" Dr. Denny Davis, 2/2015

"I would rather pay for *education* any day than pay for *ignorance*!" Dr. Denny Davis

"People don't mind change, but they resist being changed." Rev. Curtis, 2/19/15

"Many of us become *products* of our environment instead of *transcending* that environment." Dr. Denny Davis, 12/20/15

"If it were not good, you would not have bothered to insult it!" Author Unknown

"We should value people and not value things, but most often, we value things more than we value people. Things are temporary." Deacon Rodney Paul, 4/25/16

"If it is a difficult challenge, embrace it. Don't run from it!" Dorothy Sweet Calhoun, Author, 9/15

"Keep a green tree in your heart and perhaps a singing bird will come." Sophia Ojha

"A woman was trying hard to get ketchup out of the jar. During her struggle the phone rang so she asked her 4-year old daughter to answer the phone. 'mommy can't come to the phone to talk to you right now. She's hitting the bottle."

"A little girl had just finished her first week of school. 'I'm just wasting my time,' she said to her mother. 'I can't write, I can't read, and they won't let me talk!"

"A mere friend will agree with you, but a real friend will argue."

"LOVE is the key."

*** *SPIRITUAL QUOTES* ***

"There's a treasure in that trial!" Joyce Meyer, 6/9/16

"Your words can change the quality of your life." Joyce Meyer, 6/9/16

"B = Basic
 I = Instructions
 B = Before
 L = Leaving
 E = Earth"
Posted on Lilly's Fence, Zwolle, LA; Author Unknown

"If God does not BREAK a promise, shouldn't this FREE you to do His will?" Rev. Robert L. White, 1994

"EZEKIEL = Means God will strengthen."
Rev. Robert L. White, New Hope Baptist Church

"God allows us to go through some things so we can SEE HIM better."

"If you don't study to SHOW yourself approved, it will SHOW." Dr. Craig M. Smith, Chicago, III, 8/14/11

"Young sisters, pray to God and He'll send you a HERO; He won't let you be confused and end up with a ZERO!" Dr. Craig M. Smith, Chicago, Ill, 8/18/13

"Some people will stay with you as long as you have something they need. Choose your friends Biblically." Dr. Craig M. Smith, Chicago, Ill, 8/18/13

"Final words of a dying church: We've never done it this way before!" Dr. Denny Davis, Grand Prairie, TX, 2/5/12

"Doesn't matter what the chessboard of life looks like, God still has many, many moves." Dr. Denny Davis, Grand Prairie, TX, 3/4/12

"Some of us get JUST ENOUGH to get that INSPECTION STICKER!" Rev. Bobby L. Calhoun, Macedonia Baptist Church, Zwolle, LA, 5/27/12

"In Christ we are: A *life* under *new management.*" Dr. Craig M. Smith, Chicago, Ill, 8/14/11

"Don't let Faith jump out of the window and Hope jump off the truck!" Rev. Jim Anding, Faith Fellowship Baptist Church, Grand Prairie, TX, 8/28/11

"His *delay* in answering is not His *denial.*"

"The Holy rollers church, and the rollers that ain't Holy!" Dr. Walter Malone, Canaan Christian Church, Baltimore, MD, 10/18/11

"Sometimes individuals *want* the *wants*, but they don't *want* the nature of God."

"God is calling for a Christian with distinct characteristics."

"We want to get some FREQUENT FLYER MILES in the church!" Dr. Denny Davis, Grand Prairie, TX, 6/11/11

"The dollar told the dime, 'You are a small, skinny runt!' 'Yea,' said the dime, 'I might be small and skinny, but I go to church MORE often than you!" Rev. Daryl Atkinson, St. John Church Unleashed, Grand Prairie, TX, 9/25/11

"Wisdom apart from God – AIN'T!" Ruby Jefferson, St. John Church Unleashed, Grand Prairie, TX

"Sin don't care what SKIN it's in." Rev. Patricia Scott, St. John Church Unleashed, Grand Prairie, TX

"Private Praise: If you don't praise Him at home, more than likely you won't praise Him at church." Rev. Michael Allen, Dallas, TX, 4/22/12

"God uses TESTS to strengthen us." Exodus 14:31

"Don't be a SPRIRITUAL HOBO!" Rev. Michael Allen, Dallas, TX, 4/22/12

"Miracles give authenticity to the Gospel." Dr. Walter Malone, Baltimore, MD, 4/2/12

"God doesn't need your INTELLIGENCE, but He needs your FAITH." Rev. Jeremy Upton, Miami, FL, 6/24/12

"God blesses us on His standards, and not on our standards." Minister Debra Waters, St. John Church Unleashed, Grand Prairie, TX, 6/24/12

"We want a *crossless* Christianity!" Dr. Walter Malone, Baltimore, MD.

"It shouldn't take long for Kingdom Minded people to get on the SAME PAGE!" Bishop Kenneth Spears, 5/16/12

"God uses ordinary people to do extraordinary things: I KNOW I CAN!" Judges 16:15, Dr. Denny Davis, Grand Prairie, TX, 7/1/12

"Everybody is not in a 'place' to hear God." Bishop Kenneth Spears, 5/16/12

"I'm the REAL DEAL; I'm SALT!" Dr. Denny Davis, Grand Prairie, TX, 6/2/12

"The right actions must follow the right attitude." Dr. Denny Davis, Grand Prairie, TX

"As believers, we have dual citizenship – The world and the one to come." Dr. Denny Davis, Grand Prairie, TX

"We don't have power because we feed our body 3 hot meals a day but, feed our Spirit a cold snack once a week!" Dr. John Hagee, Cornerstone Church, Houston, TX, 1/10/11

"My faith: I can walk through hell with gasoline on my shoes!" Bishop Walter S. Thomas

"Sin will make you flatter than a footprint."

"Whenever God blesses your neighbor, don't get mad or distracted. It only means that He's in your neighborhood!" Rev. James Thomas, Plano, TX, 9/14/05

"In the Temple: *Heaven's flee market* going on with *Hells prices* – Mark 11:15-17." Dr. Denny Davis, Grand Prairie, TX, 8/21/11

"Born of Mary – SON: Jesus Christ = The bottom to the top; The Savior – AUTHORITY = The top to the bottom." Bishop Walter Scott Thomas, Louisville, KY, 10/17/11

"What you believe privately will be displayed publicly." Rev. Wanda Bolton Davis, St. John Church Unleashed, Grand Prairie, TX, 11/13/11

"We say: I'm waiting on God! NO. God's waiting on you!" Dr. Denny Davis, St. John Church, 2/5/12

"Apostle Paul's route was Pat and Turner: *Pat* your feet and *Turn* the corner. Aahaahahahaha!!"

"Sometimes we use prayer as a justification to Not DO something." Dr. Denny Davis, Grand Prairie, TX, 2/5/12

"Elevate your *giving* and elevate your *living*." Dr. Denny Davis, Grand Prairie, TX

"Sometimes you have to love the HELL out of folks!" Dr. Denny Davis, Grand Prairie, TX, 8/21/11

"The Spirit has helped you *with* some stuff that you use to *help* yourself to!" Bishop Walter Scott Thomas, Louisville, KY, 10/12/12

"There are **meals on wheels** but, God can provide **meals on wings**." Rev. Ellis Ford, St. John Church Unleashed, Grand Prairie, TX, 8/19/12

"It's a good day to be above ground but, it can be a good day to be below ground if you're in Christ!" Rev. Armstrong, 12/2/12

"The True Bread (Jesus) won't perish like mana did." Rev. Harrison Fields, Jr., Shreveport, LA, 7/14/99

"Sin still leaves a forwarding address." Rev. Matthew McGruder, Sunset Baptist Church, Grand Prairie, TX

"Three wrong motives for serving God = People pleasing, money, and power and authority." Rev. Michael Herbert, New Hope Baptist Church, Grand Prairie, TX, 6/6/93

"MERCY handles your past, but GRACE handles your future." Rev. David Hill, St. John Church Unleashed, Grand Prairie, TX, 1/26/14

"Sometimes our dignity keeps us from delivery." Dr. Joel Gregory, Truitt seminary, Austin, TX, 2/9/14

"GPS = God's Positioning System." Dr. Joel Gregory, 2/9/14

"MMM: MEANDERING in a MAZE of MEDIOCRITY is where God does not want us!" Rev. James Thomas, 3/16/14

"Heaven is not for STAND-BYS, but for folks with RESERVATIONS!" Rev. James Thomas, 3/16/14

"A lot of us are BIG on talking, but SMALL on walking." Dr. Denny Davis, 3/23/14

"It doesn't take anything away from *me* to celebrate *you*!" Rev. Terry Anderson, 3/5/14

"With God all U-Turns are possible." Dr. Denny Davis, 11/10/13

"God specializes in messed up people." Delvin Atkinson, 7/16/14

"When church folks get together, you have some shouters and some doubters," Delvin Atchinson, 7/16/14

"Grandmother didn't have a degree in <u>Theology</u>, but she had one in <u>Christianology</u>. Everybody ought to know who Jesus is!" Delvin Atkinson, 7/16/14

"If Jesus is the best thing that ever happened to you, He shouldn't be the best kept secret in town! Tell it!" Dr. Denny Davis, 6/8/14

"Worry yields helplessness, hopelessness, and faithlessness." Rev. Sterlin McGruder, New Hope Baptist Church, Grand Prairie, TX, 3/6/94

"Some of us PLAY in the calm and PRAY in the storm." Rev. M.E. Sargent, Dallas, TX, 8/10/93

"An undisciplined thought makes one vulnerable to the Devil." Rev. Robert L. White, New Hope Baptist Church, Grand Prairie, TX, 2/20/94

"Standing on the promises, and sitting on the premises!"

"God works through some people and works some people." Rev. Robert L. White, Grand Prairie, TX

"Satan trembles when he sees the weakest saint on his knees." Rev. Michael Herbert, 3/7/93

"We are not our own, we were bought with a price."

"If you want blessings from the Lord, grow and bloom where you are planted."

"CREATION: When the Lord created the world, He looked at it and said, 'That's good.' Then he created man, looked at him and said, 'That's good, but I believe I can do better.' So, He created woman." Mary Crowley

"You win 'em, you wet 'em, and you work 'em."
Rev. Michael Herbert, 6/6/93

"No man/woman can be wrong with his/her brother and be right with God." Rev. R.L. White, 1/15/95

"God has two rules: A dominant rule and a permissive rule." Rev. Sterlin McGruder, 10/19/94

"If you don't know God, you won't obey Him." Rev. Charles Stanley, 1/31/93

"Raise what you praise."

"Bless God for what you *have*; trust God for what you *need*."

"CH – - CH means nothing unless *UR* in it!" Rev. Sterlin McGruder's first sermon: 'God Cares.' Psalms 23, Morning Star Baptist Church, Grand Prairie, Texas, 7/15/84

"Theocracy = Under God's rule."

"Five kinds of people in church: A. The natural man; B. The babe in Christ; C. The carnal man; D. The Spirit man; and E. The disciple." Rev. Sterlin McGruder

"Shadrach, Meshach, and A –Bad – Ne – Gro (Negro)!" Rev. E.V. Hill

"The *conscience* is God's warning system. Be very happy when it warns you, but be very worried when it doesn't!" Rev. Bobby Calhoun, New Hope Baptist Church, 1/16/94

"Some people get saved because they are too old to do what they use to do." Rev. Lawrence Rayfield, New Hope Baptist Church

"YOKE = Service and submission"

"You can't have God's love without having God's judgment." Rev. R.L. White, 4/10/94

"UNITY = His word and His Spirit."

"Bemis Seat = The judgment seat of God" Rev. Sterlin McGruder

"The Lord sometimes takes us into troubled waters – not to drown us, but to cleanse us." Minister Sheilon Harrison, 1/17/93

"I need to give Satan some other address to get him off my trail!" Rev. Sterlin McGruder, 6/9/93

"Those who endure are God's little trophies of grace." Rev. Sterlin McGruder, 7/10/94

"That little sin that you thought was small enough is an open scandal in Heaven." Rev. Sterlin McGruder, 5/4/94

"Many of us can't appreciate the sunshine for we've never been through the rain." Rev. Lawrence Rayfield, 5/22/94

"Old sheep know the way. Young lambs have to find the way." Sis. Ruby Hunter, Evangelist Temple Baptist Church, Dallas, Texas, 4/15/94

"If man does not serve the God who created him, he will serve the gods he creates." Rev. Robert L. White, Grand Prairie, TX, 4/13/94

"No God - No Jesus; Know God - Know Jesus"

"If God abides, God provides and guides; God is love." Rev. Ricky Venters, Denison, Texas, 6/8/94

"Spiritual gifts=Grace gifts; we shouldn't boast about it for we didn't do it." Rev. Sterlin McGruder

"Make God the *CEO* of your business and your life." Rev. Brown

"A new level brings a new devil!" Bishop T.D. Jakes, Potter's House, Dallas, Texas

"We must *trust* Him when we can't *trace* Him!" Deacon Rodney Paul, St. John Church Sunday School, 2016

"God has brought us from *a mule's back* to *a Cadillac*!" Rev. Ellis Ford

"*Depression* happens in a wilderness place." Dr. Denny Davis

"Sometimes we pay more attention to *CNN* than to *God*." Rev. Craig Melvin

"There comes a time in our lives when God wants to release the champion in us." Dr. Denny Davis, 9/7/14

"Never be afraid when the odds are stacked against you. You never know when the stack of odds may shift in your favor." Dr. Denny Davis, 9/7/14

"When we get ten cents above bread money, we forget God!" Rev. Mitchell James, Galveston, TX

"Real worship leads to real witness."

"I'm a season ticket holder when it comes to Jesus."

"You should not try to get a fox and a chicken to be friends; make sure you don't even let the fox watch your chickens!" Rev. Lee Walton, Antioch Missionary Baptist Church, Dallas, Texas

"God is able! He put sugar in watermelon and a clock and computer in a rooster." Rev. Lee Walton

"You see my glory, but you don't know my story." Rev. Jeffrey Johnson, Love Connection Revival, St. John Church Unleashed, 2/8/17

"Preparing to preach: Give me 30 minutes and I'll give you 15 back." Rev. David Hill, St. John Church Unleashed, Grand Prairie, Texas, 2015

"You might not want to say *Amen* right now, but just say, *'Hey man.'"* Rev. David Hill, 2015

"Sin has not gotten any worse, it's just more people doing it. 'Light' has an 'ENEMY.'" Rev. Robert White, New Hope Baptist Church, 3/18/98

"We don't have to get shook up when things shake down!" Dr. Joel Gregory, from Truitt Seminary, Austin, Texas, 6/21/15

"There is no wound like the wound of a friend." Dr. Denny Davis, 4/19/15

"The best gift is forgiveness!" Dr. Denny Davis

"There are certain lesson you can't learn unless you are in a 'STORM.'" Dr. Denny Davis, 8/2/15

"God will give you the end picture, but will not give you the journey." Deacon Rodney Paul, St. John Church Unleashed, Grand Prairie, Texas, 2016

"You can't worship corporately until you have established worship privately." Rev. Fawna Taylor Jenkins, St. John Church Unleashed, 9/13/15

"Christians, Satan can oppress us, but he can't possess us." I john 4:12b

"Some people are so heavenly minded that they are no earthly good." Oliver Wendell Holmes, sr.

"God is good for the places He takes us *to*, but He is also good for the places he takes us *through*." Dr. Denny Davis, 3/16

"G = God's
 R = Riches
 A = At
 C = Christ's
 E = Expense"
Abbreviations.com, quoted by Dr. Denny Davis, 4/17/16

"We should value people and not value things, but most often, we value things more than we value people. Things are temporary." Deacon Rodney Paul, 4/25/16

"Do not use a hatchet to remove a fly from your friend's forehead!!" Chinese Proverb

"When you read Matthew 24th chapter, you get a summary of the book of Revelations." Ernestine Gilbert, Adult Women's Sunday School Class, 2016 (We will love and miss you always).

*** LIFE LESSONS***

The following pages are collections from various sources over the years and from my own writings; Authors are cited if known.

TODAY, MAKE YOUR LIFE WORTH LOVING AND LIVING!

These favorites are enlightening, enjoyable truths to live by or to be advised by.

CELEBRATE LIFE!!

Myself

I have to live with myself, and so,
I want to be fit for myself to know,
I want to be able, as days go by,
Always to look myself straight in the eye;
I don't want to stand, with the setting sun,
And hate myself for things I have done.

I don't want to keep on a closet shelf
A lot of secrets about my self,
And fool myself, as I come and go,
Into thinking that nobody else will know
The kind of a man I really am;
I don't want to dress up myself in sham.

I want to go out with my head erect,
I want to deserve all men's respect;
But here in the struggle for fame and pelf
I want to be able to like myself.
I don't want to look at myself and know
That I'm bluster and bluff and empty show.

I can never hide myself from me;
I see what others may never see;
I know what others may never know,
I never can fool myself, and so,
Whatever happens, I want to be
Self-respecting and conscience free.

Edgar A. Guest
Dorothy's favorite

Parents Should Teach Their Adult Children Responsibilities

By Dr. Adeline L. Evans

How many of you have grown children who are dependent on you for their subsistence?

Do they need you to pay their domestic bills, to take care of their children, or to bolster their spirit when they are low?

Or are you the principal care taker of your adult children? Are you sometimes lost as to how to help these grown children? Well, below are suggestions:

- Listen to them complain, but do not allow them to treat you with disrespect, such as to curse or to scream at you. If you have done your best in rearing them, do not let them hold you responsible for their condition. They have to accept responsibility for their behavior.

- Give them a helping hand if you can, but remember to look out for yourself and your future. If they cannot or will not help you now, do you think they will treat you better if you are infirmed or impoverished?

- If you lend them money or give them a favor, expect them to pay it back. By holding them to their word, you are making them responsible. Should they not pay back, do not lend them the money or the favor any more, unless they are in a life-threatening situation.

- Do not allow your children to hurt each other in front of you. If their bickering is health-threatening to you, forbid them to argue around you. They could eventually run all your friends from you and, at this time, you truly need your friends.

- Should they depend on you too much, recommend counseling and you seek it too. It takes two or more to set up co-dependency. It is not natural for a grown person to continue depending on anyone else. If you are a counselor, do not undertake counseling your children yourself.

- If your children are living with you, set rules for your house guests as you would for any other guests who extend their stay. This "guest" attitude means that you do not criticize them, in front of others nor do you accept their criticism of you. If their living with you endangers your health, ask them to leave.

- Write a will that specifically states how you want your possessions divided after your death. Leave something special to each of your children and have enough copies of the will so that at least one copy will be found.

Grown children must remember that the way they respond to parents is the same way their children will treat them.

Two Biblical sayings apply here: The first one, "Honor they father and thy mother that thy days may be long on the land which the Lord Thy God giveth thee." And the second one: "Do unto others as you would have them do unto you."

A PARENT'S PRAYER

There are so many truths stored in the hearts of parents so difficult to impart to children. Some parents find themselves without the courage or the ability to properly express such precious thoughts in conversation with children. Some parents get too emotional about it and appear to be distrustful with respect to behavior of the child. The following item is an emptying of the heart of one parent on this subject.

I GIVE you life, but cannot live it for you.
I CAN teach you things, but I cannot make you learn.
I CAN give you directions, but I cannot always be there to lead you.
I CAN allow you freedom, but I cannot account for it.
I CAN take you to church, but I cannot make you believe.
I CAN teach you right from wrong, but I can't always decide for you.

I CAN buy you beautiful clothes, but I cannot make you lovely inside.

I CAN offer you advice, but I cannot accept it for you.

I CAN give you love, but I cannot force it upon you.

I CAN teach you respect, but I can't force you to show honor.

I CAN advise you about sex, but I cannot keep you pure.

I CAN tell you the facts of life, but I can't build your reputation.

I CAN tell you about drinks, but I can't say NO for you.

I CAN warn you about drugs, but I can't prevent you from using them.

I CAN tell you about lofty goals, but I can't achieve them for you.

I CAN teach you about kindness, but I can't force you to be gracious.

I CAN advise you about friends, but I can't choose them for you.

I CAN warn you about sins, but I cannot make your morals.

I CAN love you as a child, but I cannot place you in God's family.

I CAN pray for you, but I cannot make you walk with God.

I CAN teach you about Jesus, But I cannot make Him your Savior.

I CAN teach you to OBEY, but I cannot make Jesus your Lord.

I CAN tell you how to live, but I cannot give you Eternal Life.

Women's Conference 1989, Prayer Seminar. Elder Ruby Summers University Presbyterian Church, Houston, Texas

Ten Tips On Raising Children

From the Mental Health Association of Dallas, Texas

1. Love abundantly

2. Discipline constructively

3. Spend time together

4. Tend to personal and martial needs

5. Teach right from wrong

6. Develop mutual respect

7. Really listen

8. Offer guidance

9. Foster independence

10. Be realistic

ATTITUDE

OUR SINGLE GREATEST GIFT IS THE FREEDOM TO CHOOSE OUR ATTITUDE.

YOUR ATTITUDE IS MORE IMPORTANT THAN KNOWLEDGE, EDUCATION, BACKGROUND, WEALTH, POSITION, TALENT OR APPEARANCE.

IT IS EVEN MORE POWERFUL THAN WHAT OTHER PEOPLE THINK OR SAY OR DO.

IT WILL MAKE OR BREAK A PERSON. . A TEAM. . .A COMPANY. . .A RELATIONSHIP. . .A HOME.

LIFE IS 5% WHAT HAPPENS TO ME AND 95% HOW I CHOOSE TO LOOK AND REACT TO IT.

AND SO IT IS WITH YOU . . .

YOUR ATTITUDE IS YOUR CHOICE. CHOOSE TO BE POSITIVE.

Recipe for A Happy Life

Three ounces are necessary, first of patience,
Then of repose and peace; of conscience
a pound entire is needful: Of pastimes of all sorts,
too, should be gathered as much as the hand can
hold;

Of pleasant memory and of hope three good
drachms there must be at least, but they should
moistened be with a liquor made from true
pleasures which rejoice the heart.

Then of love's magic drops, a few – but use them
sparingly, for they may bring a flame which naught
but tears can drown. Grind the whole and mix
therewith of merriment an ounce to even. Yet all this
may not bring happiness except in your orisons you
lift your voice to Him who holds the gift of health.

Margaret of Navarre (1500)

PRAYER IS REGULATED BY THE FOLLOWING PRINCIPLES:

Prayer avails only as . . .

- It is made in faith (Hebrews 11:6; Matthew 17:20),
- in the Name of Jesus (John 14:13; 15:16),
- in keeping with the Will of God (I John 5:14, 15),
- under the direction and dynamic of the Holy Spirit (Jude 20),
- by a suppliant who has confessed and renounced sin (Psalm 66:18; Isaiah 59:1-2),
- by a forgiving heart (Matthew 6:14-125),
- in a context of harmonious relationships on the human level (Matthew 5:23-24; 18:19),
- with persistence (Luke 11:5-8; 18:1-8).

From the standpoint of human responsibility, prayer is the major element in the out-working of *God's redemptive program* (I Timothy 2:1-4).

Neglect of prayer is a sin (I Samuel 12:23).

About Forgiving Others:

Bitterness is its own prison.

The sides are slippery with resentment. A floor of muddy anger stills the feet. The stench of betrayal fills the air and stings the eyes. A cloud of self-pity blocks the view of the tiny exit above.

Step in and look at the prisoners. Victims are chained to the walls. Victims of betrayal, and victims of abuse.

The dungeon, deep and dark, is beckoning you to enter. You can, you know. You've experienced enough hurt.

You can choose, like many, to chain yourself to your hurt. Or you can choose, like some, to put away your hurts before they become hates.

How does God deal with your bitter heart? He reminds you that what you have is more important than what you don't have. You still have your relationship with God. No one can take that!

He Still Moves Stones.   Author Unknown

Six Habits of Unsuccessful People

Many people have the smarts to succeed but never do. Luck has a role, but usually people make their own bad luck by regularly getting trapped in self-defeating attitudes and shoot-yourself-in-the-foot behavior. Here, from the November issue of Reader's Digest, are some of the worst traps:

1. Delusional Thinking

2. Not Producing

3. Needless Arguing

4. Dressing for Failure

5. Bad Attitudes

6. Putting First Things Last

********* *AMERICA*

So long as there are homes to which men turn
At close of day,
So long as there are homes where children are –
Where women stay,
If love and loyalty and faith be found
Across these sills,
A stricken nation can recover from
Its gravest ills.

So long as there are homes where fires burn
And there is bread,
So long as there are homes where lamps are lit
And prayers are said;
Although a people falters through the dark
And nations grope,
With GOD himself back of these homes
We still can hope.

Grace Noll Crowell

Basic Rules for Daily Living

by Thomas S. Kepler

1. Take twenty minutes by yourself at the beginning of each day.

2. Live above small troubles by losing yourself in big, worthwhile interests.

3. Grow every day; life is a game; keep your eye on the ball, rather than on the scoreboard.

4. Have power to see things through; keep remembering that most accomplishments are three-fourths drudgery, and one-fourth joy.

5. Alternate your interests. It is better to be busy than bored. Balance your life with work, play, love, and worship.

6. Be gracious to others; do kind deeds beyond the call of duty; remember that every person is fighting a battle.

7. Talk over your problems with others – with confiding friends, your doctor of medicine, your minister, your God.

8. Work and co-operate with God, praying that God will do something *through* you rather than *for* you.

Remember 6 Simple Rules To Be Happy

1. Free your mind from worries.

2. Free your heart from hatred.

3. Live simply.

4. Give more.

5. Expect less.

6. Obtain your B.A. Degree
   (Born Again Degree)

Dorothy Calhoun, Author, CALHOUNBOOKS, 2017

The Argument!

A couple drove several miles down a country road, not saying a word.

An earlier discussion had led to an argument, and neither wanted to concede their position.

As they passed a barnyard of mules and pigs, the husband Sarcastically asked, "Relatives of yours?"
"Yep," the wife replied, "In-laws."

Joke: Big Trouble!

There were two young brothers, 8 and 10 years old, who were exceedingly mischievous. Whatever went wrong in the neighborhood, it turned out they had a hand in it. Their parents were at their wits' end trying to control them.

Hearing about a pastor nearby who worked with delinquent boys, the mother suggested to her husband that she would ask the pastor to talk with the boys and he agreed.

The mother went to the pastor and made her request. He agreed, but said he wanted to see the younger boy first and alone. So, the mother sent the younger boy to the pastor.

The pastor sat the boy down across his HUGE, impressive desk. For about five minutes they just sat and stared at each other. Finally, the pastor pointed his forefinger at the boy and asked, "Young man, where is God?"

The boy looked under the desk, in the corners of the room, all around, then said nothing. Again, louder, the pastor pointed at the boy and asked, "Where is God?"

Again, the boy looked all around but said nothing. A third time, in a louder, firmer voice, the pastor leaned far across the desk and put his forefinger almost to the boy's nose, and asked, "Young man, I ask you, where is God?"

The boy panicked and ran all the way home. Finding his older brother, he dragged him upstairs to their room and into the closet, where they usually plotted their mischief. He finally said, "We're in Bi-i-i-i-i-i-g trouble.

The older boy asked, "What do you mean, 'Big trouble?'"

His brother replied, "I'm telling ya,' we're in Big trouble. God is missing and they think we did it!!"

Source: The Daily Dilly

WISDOM BRINGS BLESSINGS

My son, do not forget my teaching, but keep my commands in your heart, for they will prolong your life many years and bring you prosperity. Let love and faithfulness never leave you; bind them around your neck, write them on the tablet of your heart. Then you will win favor and a good name in the sight of God and man. Trust in the Lord with all your heart and lean not on your own understanding; in all your ways acknowledge him, and he will make your paths straight.

Proverbs 3:1-6 NIV

The Heavenly Line

In Heaven there were 2 lines.
One said, "Men who were bossed
by their wives," and the other one
said, "Men who weren't bossed by
their wives."

There was a big line for the first one,
but then the man who was
checking peoples name in
the book of life saw one man
in the other line. So, he
told the guys to wait. He asked
the man why he was in that
line. The man replied,
"My wife told me to."

The Wedding Anniversary

A couple was celebrating their 35th wedding anniversary. Both were 60 years old.

During their party, a fairy appeared to congratulate them and grant them each one wish.

The wife wanted to travel around the world. The fairy waved the wand and poof – the wife had tickets in her hand for a world cruise.

Next, the fairy asked the husband what he wanted. He said, "I wish I had a wife 30 years younger than me!"

So, the fairy picked up her wand and poof – the husband was 90!

Author unknown

The Twelve Days of Christmas

The partridge in a pear tree is *Jesus Christ.*

Two turtle doves are the *Old and New Testaments.*

Three French hens stand for *faith, hope, and love.*

The four calling birds are the four gospels – *Matthew, Mark, Luke, and John.*

The five golden rings recall the Torah or Law – *The first five books of the Old Testament – Pentateuch.*

The six geese a-laying stands for *the six days of creation.*

Seven swans a-swimming represents the sevenfold gifts of the Holy Spirit – *Prophesy, Serving, Teaching, Exhortation, Contribution, Leadership, and Mercy.*

The eight maids a-milking are *the eight beatitudes.*

Nine ladies dancing are the nine fruits of the Holy Spirit – *love, joy, peace, patience, kindness, goodness, faithfulness, gentleness, and self-control.*

The ten lords a-leaping are *the Ten Commandments.*

The eleven pipers piping stand for *the eleven faithful disciples.*

The twelve drummers drumming symbolizes *the twelve points of belief in the Apostles Creed.*

Unknown

LIVE CAREFULLY

Several years ago, a preacher from out-of-state accepted a call to a church in Houston, Texas. Some weeks after he arrived, he had an occasion to ride the bus from his home to the downtown area. When he sat down, he discovered that the driver had accidentally given him a quarter too much change.

As he considered what to do, he thought to himself, "You'd better give the quarter back. It would be wrong to keep it." Then he thought, "Oh, forget it, it's only a quarter. Who would worry about this little amount? Anyway, the bus company gets too much fare; they will never miss it. Accept it as a gift from God and keep quiet."

When his stop came, he paused momentarily at the door, then he handed the quarter to the driver and said, "Here, you gave me too much change." The driver, with a smile, replied, "Aren't you the new preacher in town? I have been thinking a lot lately about going somewhere to worship. I just wanted to see what you would do if I gave you too much change. I'll see you at church on Sunday."

When the preacher stepped off the bus, he literally grabbed the nearest light pole, held on, and said, "Oh God! I almost sold your son for a quarter!"

Our lives are the only Bible some people will ever read. This is a real scary example of how much people watch us as Christians and will put us to the test! Always be on guard for Satan, and remember, you carry the name of Christ on your shoulders when you call yourself "Christian."

Watch your thoughts; they become words.

Watch your words; they become actions.

Watch your actions; they become habits.

Watch your habits; they become character.

Watch your character; it becomes your destiny.

Author unknown

Characteristics of an Excellent Leader
(Church Leaders of Children and Adults)

1. Makes himself/herself available to talk one-on-one with children and their parents.

2. Asks for input on important matters which affect the job that one is performing.

3. Addresses problems head on in a calm, sweet, controlled, and spiritual manner.

4. Encourages new ways to solve problems as they arise.

5. Gives acknowledgments to children and staff for positive contributions.

6. Offers a positive vision for the continuing growth and development of the group/team.

7. Fosters a team spirit among the sponsors and the children/parents.

8. Is an effective communicator to the children/sponsors/parents/pastors/and others.

9. Engenders trust from children/sponsors/parents/pastors/and others.

10. Follows up on previous assignments given to the children/others.

11. Admits when a mistake has been made, and fix it, if possible, but in a way in which
God would be pleased.

12. Presents issues in a spiritual manner, and allow others involved to help with decision-making.

13. Speaks to children in a positive manner; self-control issued by the Holy Spirit is vital; children *SEE* us and *LEARN* us whatever our state.

14. Displays love at all times because God first loved us. We are His examples of *light to the world.*

15. Is born again, and full of the Holy Spirit.

Author Unknown

<u>ACCOUNTABILITY</u>

We each are responsible and accountable for
our actions, our decision, whether
good or bad, as well as our successes and
choices we make
in life. As we
journey through the corridors of
life, we must
set attainable goals, set our aims high,
and work each day to achieve all we can
and be successful
in the many challenges we meet.
It is upon US
to complete our tasks faithfully. No one
else can
do this for us. Be the best leader that you can be!
Be encouraged!

Wisdoms by Dorothy

THE GYM

An old guy – not in the best of shape – was working out in the gym when he spotted a sweet young thing.

He asked the trainer, "What machine in here should I use to impress that sweet thing over there?"

The trainer looked him up and down and said, "I would try the ATM in the lobby."

What a crush of spirit for the old man!!!!!!!!

Unknown

Mrs. Flanders

Mrs. Flanders decided to have her portrait painted. She told the artist, "Paint me with diamond earrings, a diamond necklace, emerald bracelets, and a ruby pendant."

"But you are not wearing any of those," he said.

"I know. It's in case I die before my husband. I'm sure he'd remarry, and I want her to go nuts looking for my jewelry!!"

Unknown

FUNNY!

Mildred, the church gossiper and self-appointed monitor of the church's morals, kept sticking her nose into other people's business.

Several members did not approve of her activities, but feared her enough to maintain their silence. She made a mistake, however, when she accused George, a new church member, of being an alcoholic after she saw his old pickup parked in front of the town's only bar one afternoon. She emphatically told George (and several others) that everyone seeing it there would know what he was doing.

George, a man of few words, stared at her for a moment and then just turned and walked away. He didn't explain, defend, or deny . . . He said nothing.

Later that evening, George quietly parked his pickup in front of Mildred's house. Walked home. . . And left it there all night.

You GOTTA love George!!!!

Unknown

The Future Is Now

I believe the children are our future
Teach them well and let them lead the way
Show them all the beauty they possess inside
Give them a sense of pride to make it easier
Let the children's laughter remind us how we used to
be

Everybody's searching for a hero
People need someone to look up to
I never found anyone to fulfill my needs
A lonely place to be
So, I learned to depend on me

I decided long ago, never to walk in anyone's shadow
If I fail, if I succeed
At least I'll live as I believe
No matter what they take from me
They can't take away my dignity

Because the greatest love of all is happening to me
I found the greatest love of all
Inside of me
The greatest love of all
Is easy to achieve

Lyrics - Whitney Houston

YOU ARE WHAT YOU BELIEVE ABOUT YOURSELF

One day a naturalist who was passing by asked a farmer why it was that an eagle, the monarch of all birds, should be confined to live in a barnyard with his chickens.

"Since I have given it chicken feed and trained it to be a chicken, it has never learned to fly," replied the farmer. "It behaves as chickens behave, so it is no longer an eagle."

"Still," insisted the naturalist, "it has the heart of an eagle and can surely be taught to fly,"

After talking it over, the two men agreed to find out whether this was possible. Gently, the naturalist took the eagle in his arms and said, "You belong to the sky and not to the earth. Stretch forth your wings and fly,"

The eagle, however, was confused; she did not know who she was. Seeing the chickens eating their food, she jumped down to be with them again.

Undismayed, the naturalist took the eagle on the following day up on the roof of the house and urged her again, saying, "You are an eagle. Stretch forth your wings and fly," But the eagle was afraid of the unknown and jumped down once more for the chicken food.

On the third day, the naturalist rose and took the eagle out of the barnyard to a high mountain. There he held the monarch of birds high above him and encouraged her again, saying, "You are an eagle. You belong to the sky as well as the earth. Stretch forth your wings now and fly."

Then the eagle began to tremble; slowly she stretched her wings. At last, with a triumphant cry, she soared into the heavens.

It may be that the eagle still remembers the chickens with nostalgia; it may even be that she occasionally revisits the barnyard. But she has never returned to lead the life of a chicken.

Just like the eagle, if you have learned to think of yourself as something you aren't, you can re-decide in favor of what you really are.

Jamie Glenn

SPECIAL PEOPLE

There are special people who come
Into our lives to teach us,
Support us, encourage us,
And to love us. They leave their
Imprints on our hearts and we
Will never be the same again.

Lionel Richie

Just A Minute

I have only just a minute,
Only sixty seconds in it;
Forced upon me, can't refuse it.
Didn't seek it, didn't choose it.
But it's up to me to use it,
I must suffer if I lose it,
Give account if I abuse it.
Just a tiny little minute. . .
But eternity is in it.

Author unknown

THE THINGS WE LEAVE BEHIND

Out of this life I shall never take
Things of silver and gold I make.
All that I cherish and hoard away,
After I leave, on the earth must stay.

Though I have toiled for a painting rare,
To hang on the wall, I must leave it there;
Though I call it mine and I boast its worth,
I must give it up when I leave the earth.

All that I gather and all that I keep,
I must leave behind when I fall asleep.
And I often wonder what I shall own
In that other life when I pass alone.

Shall the Great Judge learn when my task
is through, that my spirit had gathered some
riches, too? Or shall at the last it be mine to
find, that all I had worked for, I left behind.

Author unknown

In Loving We Grow

Trust in Jesus, and He will show the way
To be the very best we can be every day.
Putting Jesus first – this way we should know,
Is the only way we truly can grow.

How grateful we should be
For God's great love.
For sending His Son
To us from above.

When we give of ourselves,
Through His love we can see
That by giving ourselves
We're the best we can be.

We give thanks to our Lord,
For letting us know
That only through love
Can we really grow.

Also, We're taught,
And this is truly so –
Loving is forgiving, and
By loving we grow.

Victoria Baker Payne

DON'T QUIT!
Don't quit no matter what!

When things go wrong, as they sometimes will,
When the road you're trudging seems all uphill,
When funds are low and the debts are high,
And you want to smile but you have to sigh,
When care is pressing you down a bit,
Rest if you must, but don't you quit!

Life is queer with its twists and turns,
As everyone of us sometimes learn,
And many a failure turns about,
When he might have won if he'd stuck it out.
Don't give up, though the pace seems slow –
You might succeed with another blow.

Often the goal is nearer than
It seems to a faint and faltering man;
Often the struggler has given up
When he might have captured the victor's cup,
And he learned too late, when the night slipped down,
How close he was to the golden crown.

Success is failure turned inside out -
The silver tint of the clouds of doubt,
And you never can tell how close you are -
It may be near when it seems afar;
So, stick to the fight when you're hardest hit –
It's when things seem worse that you mustn't quit!!!

Author unknown

Nelson Mandela

by

Monique Sylvia Diane Mitchell
Age 10
My granddaughter

My old feller was born in 1918.
The South African people were poor, but
Proud of Nelson and all he did for them.
When he died, they grieved more.
They threw their fists up in the air,
angry and sad that their leader was gone.
But the whites, you can tell, didn't really care.
Not one tear came out of their eyes –
not one from any of them!
He did all that he did for freedom
and he did it for love, but
they guessed it just wasn't enough.
Nelson Mandela was finally free.
Nelson Mandela did it for me!!

A SHOP LIFTER

A woman was arrested for shop lifting.
When she went before the judge, he asked her,
"What did you steal?" She replied, "A can of
peaches."

The judge asked why she had stolen them and
she replied that she was hungry. The judge
asked her how many peaches were in the can.
She replied, "6." The judge then said,
"I will give you 6 days in jail."

Before the judge could actually pronounce the
punishment, the woman's husband spoke
up and asked the judge if he could say
something. The judge said, "What is it?"

The husband said, "She also stole a can of peas!"

Rick Thomas

The Collard Greens

An old Black man lived alone in the country.
He wanted to dig his yearly collard green garden, but it was always very hard work for him because the ground was hard. His only son, Junebugg Jankins III, who used to help him, was in prison. The old man wrote a letter to his son and described his predicament.

Dear Junebugg Jankins III:
I am feeling pretty bad because it look like I won't be able to plant my collard green garden this year. I'm just getting too old to be digging up a garden plot. If you were here my troubles would be over. I know you would dig the plot for me.
Love Dad

A few days later, he received a letter from his son.

Dear Daddy Jankins. Whatever you do, don't dig up that garden. That's where I buried the BODIES! Love Junebugg Jankins III

At 4a.m. the next morning, FBI agents and local police arrived and dug up the entire area without finding any bodies. They apologized to the old man and left. That same day the old man received another letter from his son.

Dear Daddy Jankins. You can go ahead and plant the collard greens now. That's the best I could do under the circumstances. Love Junebugg III.

Author unknown

SHINGLES

Bubba had Shingles. Those of us who spend much time in a doctor's office should appreciate this! Doesn't it seem more and more that physicians are running their practices like an assembly line? Here's what happened to Bubba:

Bubba walked into a doctor's office and receptionist asked him what he has. Bubba said, "Shingles." So, she wrote down his name, address, medical insurance number and told him to have a seat.

Fifteen minutes later, a nurse's aide came out and asked Bubba what he had.
A half hour later, a nurse came in and asked Bubba what he had. Bubba said, "Shingles." So, the nurse gave Bubba a blood test, a blood pressure test, an electrocardiogram, and told Bubba to take off all his clothes and wait for the doctor.

An hour later, the doctor came in and found Bubba sitting patiently in the nude and asked Bubba what he had. Bubba said, "Shingles." The doctor asked, "Where?"

Bubba said, "Outside on the truck. Where do you want me to unload 'em??"

Ahhahahahhahahah!!!

Author unknown

A Parable of Two Frogs

Two frogs lived on the edge of a remote pond. One particularly dry summer, the pond dried up completely and the frogs had to search elsewhere for water and food.

So, one morning, they set out before the sun was above the horizon. They traveled all day across a hot, dusty field, through the shadow of a grove of trees, and over the rocky bed of a dried-up stream. They traveled throughout the night and, finally, late the next day, as they crested the top of a hill, they sighted a farm in the valley below.

The farmer was just finishing his chores. He had fed the chickens and the pigs and milked the cows. However, as he left the barn, he forgot to take with him the last pail of fresh, warm milk.

When the farmer was gone, the two tired frogs made their way down the hill, sensing their journey was coming to a successful end. They saw the bucket of warm milk as they hopped through the door of the barn. They found a low edge and were able to hop over the side of the bucket into the creamy, nourishing dinner.

The two frogs drank until their stomachs were full and their thirst was quenched. Only then did they discover that the milk was too deep for them to touch bottom, and the sides of the bucket were too high for them to climb out. Their survival depended on swimming continuously.

Before long, the stress of the journey and the weight of their full stomachs began to tell. Swimming became more difficult and their bodies were craving sleep.

The desperateness of their situation and the weight of their exhaustion eventually led one of the frogs to admit to his friend that he was ready to stop swimming and allow himself to drown. But his friend wouldn't hear of it. He urged his companion to keep trying; after all, they had come too far to quit now.

Before long, the situation reversed. The second frog was ready to quit, but with the encouragement and urging of his friend, he kept swimming. And, so, they passed the night.

In the morning, when the farmer entered the barn, he found the forgotten bucket of milk and, to his surprise, he saw the two frogs sound asleep, floating on a pad of butter.

This parable contains many messages useful to our lives:

1. First, when things aren't going the way we want, we need to take the initiative and go search for the answers we need.

2. Second, our search can be an adventurous journey, not just a trip.

3. Third, what appears to be the solution we seek can later become the problem.

4. Fourth, the problem we encounter may eventually offer our solution.

5. Fifth, stay close to your friends. They encouragement they offer may give you the strength to prevail.

6. Finally, don't give up. Your struggle may be creating a helpful and unexpected answer to your circumstances.

- Remember, God has the last word in how any situation in our lives will turn out regardless of the circumstances.

Author unknown

WISDOMS,

CHOICES, and EXPERIENCES

have provided me the opportunity to receive several awards and recognitions during my careers as an educator and as an author:

- **The first African-American teacher of South Grand Prairie High School**

- **The first elementary Master Art Specialist: Designed the curriculum and executed it by piloting the first elementary art program for the district**

- **Named Who's Who Among America's Teachers**

- **Named All American Scholar at Texas Woman's University's Education Department, Denton, Texas**

- **Named Unsung Hero three times: Grand Prairie ISD, Grand Prairie NAACP, and the ETA PHI BETA Sorority, Dallas Chapter, Dallas, Texas**

- **Distinguished Alumnus Award for Memorial Service Director, J.S. Clark High School Alumni Convention, Louisiana**

- **PTA Lifetime Membership, Grand Prairie ISD**

- **Honored by GPISD as a local author by their purchase of Six Bees for Children and The Princesses of Arvallay for every elementary school's library in the district**

- **The White House: 2016 official letter from President and Mrs. Barack Obama who shared commendations and accolades after receiving the four copies of my published books**

I'm not finished yet!!!!! Smiles!!!